Sc√m

THE SCIENCE MUSEUM BOOK OF AMAZING FACTS

n or before
ow.

EXPLORATION

Anthony Wilson once spent an exciting month exploring the glaciers and hot springs of Iceland. He then spent several years exploring the upper atmosphere by sending up scientific gadgets dangling from high-altitude balloons. He is a writer and teacher who for many years was Head of Education at the Science Museum in London, where he set up the popular hands-on gallery Launch Pad. He is now helping establish a Hands-on Science Centre in a former astronomical observatory at Herstmonceux in Sussex.

Many of the amazing facts in this book were inspired by exhibits in the SCIENCE MUSEUM in London. It is home to many of the greatest treasures in the history of science, invention and discovery, and there are also hands-on galleries where you can try things out for yourself. If you live in the science Museum's out way Museum in York and the Photography, Fil Bradford.

Monaghan County Libraries

5407000081 1354

Copyright © 1997 Anthony Wilson
Illustrations copyright © 1997 Christine Roche

Published by Hodder Children's Books 1997
The right of Anthony Wilson to be identified as the Author and
the right of Christine Roche to be identified as the Illustrator of the Work
has been asserted by them in accordance with the
Copyright, Designs and Patents Act 1988

10 9 8 7 6 5 4 3 2 1

All rights reserved. No part of this publication may be
reproduced, stored in a retrieval system, or transmitted,
in any form or by any means without the prior written
permission of the publisher, nor be otherwise circulated
in any form of binding or cover other than that in which
it is published and without a similar condition being
imposed on the subsequent purchaser.

A Catalogue record for this book is available
from the British Library

ISBN 0 340 69000 3

Designed by Fiona Webb
Cover illustration by Ainslie MacLeod

Hodder Children's Books
A division of Hodder Headline plc
338 Euston Road
London NW1 3BH

Printed and bound in Great Britain by
Mackays of Chatham PLC, Chatham, Kent.

sci √m

THE SCIENCE MUSEUM BOOK OF AMAZING FACTS

EXPLORATION

ANTHONY WILSON

ILLUSTRATED BY CHRISTINE ROCHE

*Hodder
Children's
Books*

a division of Hodder Headline plc

E28.728/GEO

Contents

I SPY, I SPY WITH MY LITTLE EYE...

Travelling far and wide

A thousand years ago there were no maps of the world, because no one knew what the world looked like. Most people never strayed more than a few kilometres from the place where they were born. But a few people were more adventurous. They were the first explorers, brave enough to set out for unknown places, not knowing what they might find there. They brought back tales of strange and wonderful places, which encouraged more explorers to follow in their footsteps. And so the gaps in the map of the world were gradually filled in.

Some explorers were looking for wealth. They brought back rare and valuable goods — such as silk cloth, spices and precious stones — to sell to people at home. Later there were scientist explorers, who roamed the world in search of unusual plants and animals.

And a few people became explorers for a different reason. They simply longed for the challenge and excitement of going to places where no one had been before. One of them, a mountaineer named George Mallory, summed it up very neatly. When asked why he wanted to risk his life trying to reach the top of Mount Everest, he gave one simple reason: 'Because it is there.'

FIRST EXPLORER?

The first known explorer was an Egyptian called Harkhut, who lived more than 4000 years ago. Like many explorers Harkhut was keen to buy things from people he met on his journeys. After one expedition up the Nile valley he returned with all sorts of valuable goods – ivory (elephant tusks), ebony (a special hard wood), incense (to burn to make a pleasant smell), and rare animal skins, all carried on the backs of 300 asses. From another trip into the depths of Africa he came back with a live pygmy – a member of an African group where nobody is more than about 1.5 metres tall. The King of Egypt was fascinated to meet such a small person. We don't know what the pygmy thought about meeting the King of Egypt.

SMALL IS BEAUTIFUL, MATE!

SQUARE EARTH

People in ancient Peru thought the Earth might be square, like a box, with a roof where their god lived. And in ancient Egypt they pictured an egg-shaped Earth, guarded at night by the moon – like a mother goose guarding her own eggs. But the Greeks, more than 2000 years ago, had the right idea. Many Greeks thought the world was a sphere (like a ball), and they had the evidence of their own eyes to prove it. They watched eclipses of the moon, and saw that the Earth makes a shadow that is curved at the edge – just the sort of shadow a sphere would make.

WE ARE HERE.

FOUR-EYED PEOPLE

People with four eyes, and people with back-to-front feet once lived in remote parts of the world. At least, that's what the Roman, Gaius Solinus, said in a book written more than 1700 years ago. Solinus collected many 'traveller's tales', but wasn't worried about whether they were true or not. His book also mentions people with dog's heads in Ethiopia, and ants the size of dogs in another part of Africa. He even describes a race of 'unipods', people with only one leg, but so long that they could use their giant foot as a sunshade by holding it over their heads. Needless to say, none of these strange creatures really existed.

HERE BE MONSTERS

Early maps of the world included man-eating monsters and other frightening creatures. Map-makers often knew how to draw the coastline of places such as Africa, but they did not know what lay inside the continent. So instead of leaving it blank, they filled it with pictures of elephants, tigers and even stranger imaginary beasts. Sometimes the empty spaces were labelled 'Terra Incognita', which is Latin for 'unknown territory'. Later, after explorers had made their way inland, the gaps in the maps were filled in.

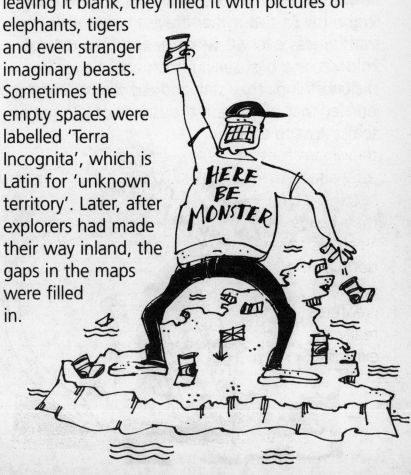

LONG TIME NO SEE

Imagine coming home after more than twenty years away. Would your friends and relations know who you were? That was the problem for Marco Polo and his father and uncle when they returned to Venice in the year 1295. Marco was only seventeen when they set off on a journey to the Far East. But their travels lasted so long that he was over 40 when he returned. Marco Polo wrote a best-selling book about the exciting things they saw and did on the 24-year journey that took them thousands of kilometres across Asia to China.

But he later said this book only told *half* the truth; he thought that if he had included the rest of his amazing adventures, nobody would have believed any of it.

A PRESENT FOR THE EMPEROR

For many years China was a closed country that people from outside could not visit. But an Italian priest called Matteo Ricci used a clever idea to get inside the imperial capital, Peking, in the year 1601. His idea was to send the emperor a present, consisting of two clocks. The Emperor, Wan-li, was a strange man, who was amazed by the clocks and loved to listen to the little bell that chimed the hours. But he hated meeting people. So to find out who had sent the clocks he allowed Ricci into Peking, and asked an artist to paint a portrait of him so the Emperor could see what he looked like without having to meet him. Ricci had made the 8000-kilometre journey from Italy to China to work there as a teacher and preacher. After his success with the clocks he stayed in Peking for nine years, and even wrote several books in Chinese.

TREE-HUNTER

If John Tradescant hadn't gone plant-hunting in America in 1637, London might look very different today. Tradescant was looking for new sorts of plant that don't normally grow in Britain. One of the plants he sent back to his father in London was a plane tree. It is said that the many thousands of large planes that today line the streets of London and other great cities are descended from this tree. Plane trees stand up to dirt and pollution very well because they have leathery leaves which wash clean when it rains.

SHOCKING DISCOVERY

Which explorer has the most places named after him? The answer is probably the German naturalist Alexander von Humboldt. Look up 'Humboldt' in the index of an atlas and you should find a river, a glacier, a mountain, an ocean current and several towns, all named after him. In fact it is said that more than a thousand places in the world carry his name. And there's even a Humboldt crater on the Moon.

In 1799 Humboldt set off on a five-year journey that took him more than 9500 kilometres through Central and South America, finding out all he could about the wildlife and geography there. One of the unusual creatures he found out about was the dangerous electric eel – a fish that can stun its prey by giving it a 650-volt electric shock.

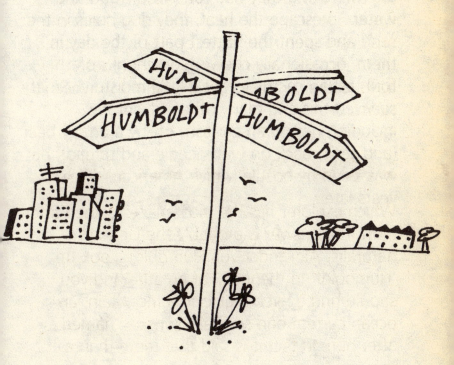

HEADS IN THE SAND

The first explorers to reach California overland survived by burying themselves up to their necks in sand. In 1826 Jedediah Smith and his companions were crossing the region called the Mojave Desert – the hottest and driest part of North America. There was no shade anywhere and they had run out of food and water. To escape the heat, they dug holes in the sand and spent the hottest part of the day in them, occasionally chewing on chunks of foul-tasting cactus to get a little moisture. Smith survived this and many other adventures, including having an ear torn off by a grizzly bear (and sewn back on with needle and thread), but was killed by hostile Native Americans a few years later.

GENTLE GIANTS

Don't jump to conclusions. That's the message we learn from the first European who ever saw a gorilla. Paul du Chaillu was exploring in West Africa in the 1850s when he heard about the giant ape. He described it as fierce and untameable, and terrifying to everyone who sees it, but today we know he was mistaken: gorillas are shy, gentle, giants. They don't eat meat and are only dangerous if you do something to upset them. Sadly, du Chaillu was also the first white man to shoot a gorilla. Today there are so few gorillas left in the wild that they are listed as an endangered species.

ARG-HHH MEAT!

- GORILLA -

SMOKE THAT THUNDERS

Imagine suddenly coming across a waterfall twice as high and twice as wide as Niagara, and which no one from Europe has ever set eyes on before. That's what happened to the Scottish explorer David Livingstone on 16 November 1855. As he made his way across Africa, following the route of the great Zambezi River, he saw a cloud of smoke in the distance and heard the sound of thunder. As he came closer he found the smoke was spray from the mighty waterfall and the thunder was the sound of 1000 tonnes of water cascading over it every second. Livingstone named the falls 'Victoria' after the Queen of England, but the African people have a much better name for it, 'Mosi-oa-Tunya', which means 'the smoke that thunders'.

DOCTOR LIVINGSTONE I PRESUME!

Yes – those famous words really were spoken, by an explorer in the depths of Africa in 1871. Four years earlier the great David Livingstone had set off to explore the region around Lake

Tanganyika (between the countries we now call Tanzania and the Congo). But nothing had been heard from him for several years, and people at home were worried. So a newspaper reporter called Henry Stanley was sent to Africa to search for Livingstone. After nearly eight months he finally found him, and uttered the famous words – even though it couldn't possibly have been anyone but Livingstone as there wasn't another European within a few hundred kilometres. In those days it wasn't polite to get over-excited, but what would *you* say, when you finally found someone who had been lost for nearly four years?

DR. LIVINGSTONE, I PRESUME...

WELL, IT AIN'T ELVIS PRESLEY...

CROSSING AUSTRALIA

Don't take camels and horses on the same
expedition. That's what Robert Burke and
William Wills discovered when they set off from
Melbourne in 1860, at the start of the first ever
attempt to cross Australia from south to north.
The horses were so scared of the camels that
they misbehaved and had to be kept apart from
them. The animals carried all the expedition's
luggage, which included books to read, rum for
the camels to drink and 120 mirrors to give as
presents to any Aborigines they might meet.

Some members of the party stopped behind at a base camp, where they found a new problem – a plague of rats that kept stealing their food. In the end they found the only way to keep the food safe was to hang it from the trees by pieces of string.

EIGHT HOURS TOO LATE

MONAGHAN COUNTY
£28.728/GEO
LIBRARY

'Dig – 3 feet North-West'. That was the message that Burke and Wills found when they staggered back to their base camp four months later, starving and exhausted after their double crossing of Australia. But where were the people, and the vital food supplies, that should have been at the base? When Burke and Wills did what the message said, they dug up a bottle with a letter inside. It said that the people at the camp, after waiting four months for the explorers to return, had left on the morning of that same day. If Burke and Wills had got back just eight hours earlier they would have been rescued. They found a small supply of food, buried next to the message in the deserted camp, but it did not save them from starving to death before they could reach the nearest inhabited place – which had the unfortunate name of 'Mount Hopeless'.

LUCKY BREAK

A broken rope saved Edward Whymper's life on the first ever successful climb of the Matterhorn. The Matterhorn, in the Swiss Alps, is a huge lump of rock jutting up to a height of 4478 metres above sea level. Whymper, with six other men, reached its summit on the afternoon of 14 July 1865. On the way down, one person slipped on the ice and began to fall. Because the men were roped together, he dragged three others with him, and all four fell 1200 metres to their deaths. Luckily for Whymper and his two Swiss guides the 'life-line' snapped before they too could be dragged over the precipice, and they lived to see another day.

HOT SPOT

A few years later, Whymper was in South America. When he set up camp near the top of Mount Cotopaxi in 1880, his tent began to melt. Cotopaxi, in Ecuador, is the world's highest active volcano. The rocks around its steaming summit were hot enough to melt the rubber sheet that Whymper used for the floor of his tent. Whymper was studying mountain sickness, an illness that effects people when

they go to high places, above about 2500 metres. The air is thinner at these heights, and shortage of oxygen brings on breathlessness, dizziness, headaches and stomach upsets. The effects usually wear off after a few days. (To find out how to avoid mountain sickness, look at **Gas bags**, on page 96)

CAUGHT IN A TRAP

When Mary Kingsley fell into an elephant trap she was saved by her long black skirt. In 1894 Mary was exploring a part of Africa where no European had been before. The elephant trap was a huge pit, dug by the Africans who lived nearby. It had bamboo sticks and leaves over the top to make it invisible, and the bottom of the pit was covered with sharp wooden spikes.

Mary was bruised when she fell into the trap, but the thickness of her skirt stopped her being wounded by the spikes. Her African guide cut down a length of creeper – a long rope-like plant – and used it to pull her out.

FUNNY LOOKING ELEPHANT

GRIM DISCOVERY

Mary Kingsley travelled alone at a time when it was very rare for women to go exploring at all. But she was extremely brave and resourceful. Soon after the adventure with the elephant trap she stayed the night at the house of a chief of the Fang tribe, the native Africans who lived in the area. She looked inside a bag hanging on the wall of her room, and made a truly gruesome discovery. It contained parts of humans, such as ears, eyes and toes. At that time, in the 1890s, the Fang people were cannibals, and these were some of their left-overs. Mary Kingsley probably didn't sleep much that night, but she survived the journey and returned safely to England.

TEA BREAK

Suppose you are exploring central Africa, and need to know how high above sea level your camp is. How can you find out – without even looking outside your tent? It sounds impossible, but it's not. All you have to do is make a cup of tea. When the water boils, use a thermometer to measure its temperature. Then use the rule

'for every 300 metres you go up, the boiling point of water comes down by 1 °C' The method was used more than a century ago by explorers trying to find the source of the River Nile in Africa (*see* **Mountain Breakfast** *page 29*).

EXPLORING IN STYLE

An American explorer in the 1920s insisted on having his evening meal on a table with a clean tablecloth – wherever he was in the world. He would usually dress up for dinner in a smart white shirt, jacket and tie, and always took a bath – in his folding bathtub – beforehand. Even in the most out-of-the-way places he expected his servants to cook him delicious Austrian dishes. The explorer's name was Joseph Rock, and he was a plant-hunter who set out to find a rare tree whose seeds were said to be useful for treating the dreadful disease of leprosy. He eventually found the tree, and collected its seeds, in the remote forests of Burma.

FIRST AT THE TOP?

The first people to reach the top of Mount Everest looked for signs that someone had been there before them. Edmund Hillary from New Zealand and Tenzing Norgay from Nepal reached the highest point on Earth in May 1953. They took photographs and left presents for the gods. Then they searched for anything that might have been left there by two earlier British climbers, George Mallory and Andrew Irvine, but didn't find anything. On an expedition in 1924 Mallory

and Irvine were seen close to the summit of
Everest. But they never returned and their
bodies have not been found. It's just possible
they conquered Everest 29 years before Hillary
and Tenzing; we'll probably never know for sure.

MOUNTAIN BREAKFAST

You can't have a boiled egg for breakfast at the top of Mount Everest – because boiling water isn't hot enough up there. Everyone knows that water normally boils at 100 °C, but that's not always true. When you climb a mountain the air pressure around you gets less, because there is less air pressing down on you from above. And at lower air pressure, water boils more easily. At the top of Snowdon, the highest mountain in England and Wales, water boils at only 97 °C. Everest is so high that water boils at only 65 °C at the top, and that's not hot enough to cook an egg. However long you boiled it for, the albumen (transparent part of a raw egg) would never turn white and become solid.

COLOURED MAPS

Some explorers make maps, and almost all explorers use them. But do you know how many different colours are needed to fill in a map? It took a computer six weeks of non-stop work to answer that simple question. Look at a map of the counties of Britain, or the states of the USA. How many colours are needed to colour it so that every county, or state, is a different colour from the ones next to it?

The answer is just four. Three colours are not enough, and no one has ever managed to invent a map which needs five different colours. (You can test this by inventing some maps of your own and colouring them in.)

In 1976 two American mathematicians proved that it's impossible to invent a map that needs more than four colours – but the proof was so complicated it took 1000 hours of computer time to work it out, and they needed a 170-page book to explain how they did it. So if you can invent a map that really needs five colours, you'll be famous!

MODERN MONSTERS

Strange monsters are still sometimes reported by explorers in remote parts of the world. Some people believe a huge creature called a 'Yeti' or 'Abominable Snowman' lives in the high Himalayan mountain region. And a large hairy animal, called 'Bigfoot', is supposed to live in the woods and mountains of north-west America. Bigfoot is said to be up to 4.5 metres tall and to walk around on two legs, like a human, giving off a horrible smell. But no one has ever taken a photograph of these creatures, and most scientists agree that they don't really exist.

YETI

YETI
DOESN'T
EXIST
OFFICIAL

SEARCHING FOR MEDICINES

Modern explorers still go to remote parts of the world looking for new medicines to cure diseases. They talk to people who live in these regions, and ask them how they make their own medicines, using plants and trees that grow in the area. Then the explorers bring back samples of these plants and trees which scientists can test to see if useful medicines can be extracted from them.

Medicines discovered in this way range from aspirin to a powerful anti-cancer drug extracted from the Rosy Periwinkle plant that grows on the island of Madagascar in the Indian Ocean.

Some possible medicine-plants grow in tropical Rain Forests that are being destroyed because people need the land to grow crops. So scientists must race to 'discover' these plants before it's too late.

Quiz

1 Terra Incognita is the Latin for . . .
a) Beware of the dog
b) Unknown territory
c) Keep off the grass

2 Marco Polo is famous for . . .
a) Writing a book about his travels
b) Introducing peppermints into Italy
c) Discovering America

3 To survive the heat in the Mojave Desert, Jedediah Smith . . .
a) Used a cactus as a sunshade
b) Buried himself in the sand
c) Hitched a lift from a grizzly bear

4 Mosi-oa-Tunya is an African name for . . .
a) The Victoria Falls
b) Dr David Livingstone
c) A runaway elephant

5 The first men to cross Australia from North to South were called . . .
a) Smith and Jones
b) Wallace and Gromit
c) Burke and Wills

6 Edward Whymper was one of the first people to . . .
a) Swim the Channel
b) Climb the Matterhorn
c) Fall into a volcano

7 Mary Kingsley was a famous woman explorer who . . .
a) Stayed with cannibals in Africa
b) Rode an elephant in India
c) Went over Niagara falls in a barrel

8 You can't boil an egg at the top of Mount Everest because . . .
a) Chickens can't lay eggs at that height
b) It would upset the mountain-gods
c) Water boils at too low a temperature there

9 Yeti and Bigfoot are the names of . . .
a) The first people to climb Mount Everest
b) Two rivers in America
c) Frightening creatures that probably don't exist

10 Rosy Periwinkle is the name of . . .
a) The first woman to explore Australia
b) A rare bird found in South America
c) A plant that provides a useful medicine

The ends of the earth

In 1900 there were few places left on Earth to explore. The Poles — North and South — were two of them. Reaching the North Pole meant trekking over the treacherous floating ice of the Arctic Ocean. The South Pole was even harder to reach, at the centre of the huge uninhabited continent of Antarctica. Bitter cold and other dangers claimed many lives, but by the end of 1911 explorers had reached both Poles and survived.

In earlier years many expeditions had sailed round the edge of the Arctic Ocean looking for a way round the north of Canada that would be a short cut to countries like China and Japan. Sometimes their ships were crushed by floating ice, or trapped in solid ice for years at a time.

Since 1911 other explorers have reached the Poles, sometimes travelling by 'snowmobile', aeroplane, or even submarine. In Antarctica there is so much to study that permanent bases have been set up where scientists from many countries can live and work. People live quite comfortably at the South Pole itself, some of them even staying there through the bitter winter months when the sun never rises above the horizon.

HOW MANY POLES?

How many Poles has the Earth? Most people say there are two, the North Pole and the South Pole, but actually there are many more. For example there are at least three different North Poles. Look at a globe of the Earth. The place where all the lines of longitude meet at the top is called the *Geographic* North Pole. It's the point that explorers try to reach. But the *Instantaneous* North Pole is slightly different. It's the place where the Earth's axis (the line it spins round) meets the surface.

Because the Earth wobbles as it spins this Pole moves slowly over an area of a few square metres. Then there's the *Magnetic* North Pole, which is the place that a compass needle points to. At present it is in Northern Canada, several hundred kilometres away from the other North Poles. And there are just as many South Poles too.

POLES APART

The Earth's two Poles are quite different. The Geographic North Pole is in the middle of the sea. The water is 4 kilometres deep there. The climate is so cold that the ocean is covered with a floating island of pack-ice all year round. The Geographic South Pole is on land, part of a continent twice the size of Australia, called Antarctica. The Pole itself is on a frozen plateau nearly 3 kilometres above sea level, which is more than twice the height of the tallest mountain in Britain. No one has actually touched the Earth's surface at the South Pole because it is permanently covered with a layer of ice more than 1.6 kilometres thick.

AURORA

Explorers in arctic and antarctic regions sometimes see amazing coloured shapes in the night
sky – and not just when they've had too much
to drink! The displays, called aurorae, often
form moving curtains and bands of red and
green light, and sometimes last for hours at a
time. They are caused when electric particles
shooting out from the Sun crash into the Earth's
upper atmosphere. Just occasionally people in
northern parts of Britain can see the aurorae –
also known as 'Northern Lights' – too.

LOST IN THE ICE

When one Arctic expedition went missing in the
1840s, 40 more expeditions set out to look for
it. The lost expedition was led by Sir John
Franklin. He set out from Britain in May 1845
with more than 100 men on board two ships,
the *Erebus* and the *Terror*. Their aim was to find
the North-West Passage, a sea-route from the
Atlantic to the Pacific round the north of North
America where the sea is frozen solid for much
of the year. Three months after they set out,
Franklin's ships were spotted in the Arctic by a

passing whaling-ship. After that they vanished. Several years passed, and people at home began to get very worried.

CLUE FROM THE INUITS

In 1848 a reward of £20,000 was offered to anyone who could rescue Sir John Franklin and his men alive from the Arctic, or £10,000 for anyone who brought back news of their fate. Over the next ten years forty separate expeditions went to look, some travelling overland from Northern Canada, and others by ship and then sledge across the ice. But no one knew exactly where to search. In 1854, John Rae, an explorer returning from Northern Canada, brought interesting news. He had met some Inuit people who told him that a few years before they had seen a party of 40 white men dragging a sledge, suffering from cold and starvation. The Inuits showed Rae some things they had got from the white men. These included spoons from Franklin's expedition.

GRISLY TRAIL

The sad end to the story came a few years later. In 1859 yet another expedition set out, led by

Captain M'Clintock and paid for by Franklin's wife, Jane. On an island in the Arctic they found a pile of stones. Inside it was a message which told the whole story. After a year of exploring, Sir John Franklin's ships had become trapped in the ice. After another year, Franklin and others had died. After yet another year the ships were crushed by the pressure of the ice. The few men still alive gave up waiting for rescue and set off to walk back to safety. A grisly trail of skeletons, found by M'Clintock's party, showed how far the last survivors of Franklin's tragic expedition had got before they finally collapsed and died, starving and exhausted.

WANDERING POLE

Which way does a compass point when you're at the Magnetic North Pole? The answer is 'straight downwards'. (You have to use a special compass called a 'dip circle' which can point up or down, because a normal compass can only point horizontally.) The explorer James Ross was the first person to find the exact position of the Magnetic North Pole, in 1831. But 70 years later, when Roald Amundsen tracked down the Pole, he found it in a different place. So who was right? We now know that the Magnetic Pole moves at a rate of a few kilometres every year, so Ross and Amundsen had both been correct.

UP THE POLE?

The first explorer to visit the Geographic North Pole may have gone to the wrong place. With one American and four Inuit companions, the American, Robert Peary, reached the Pole on 6 April 1909 – or so he claimed. Not everyone believed him. The expedition travelled across floating ice, and that may have carried them off course. Some of the people who have studied Peary's original diaries think he may have made mistakes when he worked out his position, and

possibly ended up about 50 kilometres away from the actual Pole. Probably we will never know for sure.

COLD COMFORT

GET THE BEER YOU GUYS— WE'VE ARRIVED!

When a party of Americans reached the North Pole in 1959 they took a juke box, a drinks machine, and a complete cinema with them. And they didn't have to walk any distance to get there, because they reached the Pole *from underneath*. The crew of the submarine *Skate* travelled in style, eating their meals with silver knives and forks from tables with white table-cloths. The specially-strengthened submarine travelled to the Pole beneath the ice, and broke

its way through to the surface when it got there. A Russian nuclear submarine repeated the feat soon afterwards, but was said to leak radioactivity. Its crew drank plenty of vodka because they thought it would protect them from the radioactivity – a nice idea, but without a grain of truth!

POLAR RIDDLE

Try this on your friends: You are lost in the middle of a snowy landscape. You find a signpost which has four arms, all pointing in different directions. All four arms say the same thing 'To the North Pole'. Where are you? The only possible answer is: at the South Pole. It's the only place on Earth where you could set off in any direction, and if you kept on going in a straight line you would eventually get to the North Pole – but only after travelling half-way round the world.

CHANGE OF PLAN

When explorer Roald Amundsen set off on his most famous expedition in 1910, only five people knew where he was going. For several years Amundsen had been planning to be the first person to reach the Geographic North Pole. But before he set off, the American explorer Robert Peary announced he had already got there. So Amundsen decided to head south instead. But he kept his plans secret from everyone except a few close friends, until after they left Norway. Amundsen's expedition was a success. He and four other Norwegians reached the South Pole on 14 December 1911, the first people ever to go there.

TOO LATE AT THE POLE

When Robert Scott's British expedition reached the South Pole in 1912 they had the biggest disappointment of their lives. Amundsen had got there first, just 35 days earlier. Scott's ill-fated party had set off across the frozen continent with the help of motor-driven sledges as well as sledges pulled by dogs and Siberian ponies. But the motors soon broke down, and later the ponies had to be shot and the dog

teams sent back. After an 81-day trek, Scott and his four companions reached the Pole, pulling their own sledges. On the return journey, bad weather held them up, and all five died from cold and exhaustion. Later their bodies were found – just eighteen kilometres from a food-supply base that would have saved them.

DOG-POWER

Dogs were the secret of Amundsen's successful expedition to the South Pole – but they weren't just for towing sledges. Amundsen took 42 Greenland Eskimo dogs on his expedition. Harnessed in teams, these wolf-like creatures were tough enough to pull a half-tonne sledge 80 kilometres in a day. But Amundsen had other plans for them too. Part-way through the journey he had 24 of the dogs shot, to provide a good supply of meat, for the humans as well as for the remaining dogs. Dog-lovers in Britain were shocked when Amundsen later said 'We treated ourselves to dog cutlets ... excellent, absolutely excellent'.

MOVING THE POLE

What's the most unusual job you've ever heard of? Being the scientist who moves the South Pole must be one of them. The exact position of the Geographic South Pole is fixed by a marker stuck into the thick layer of ice that covers Antarctica. This ice is moving very slowly, and carries the pole-marker along with it. So once a year, on 31 December, someone has the job of picking up the marker and 'moving the South Pole', by about nine metres, to take it back to

the correct place. On Christmas Eve people who live in the scientific station at the Pole hold a 'Race-around-the-World'. The course is three kilometres long and takes them in a circuit round the South Pole three times.

HUNTING FOR METEORITES

Antarctica is the best place in the world to look for meteorites – rocks and stones that hit the Earth from space. Although meteorites are very rare, in Antarctica they have collected in the ice

over many thousands of years, and they're easy to see against the white snowy surface. In 1991 explorers in Victoria Land (part of Antarctica) found 264 meteorites in a single expedition. Astronomers think that most meteorites are bits of miniature planets called asteroids, which circle the Sun between the orbits of Mars and Jupiter. When asteroids crash together or fall apart, smaller lumps of rock are chipped off. Some of these may spiral towards the Earth and hit the ground as meteorites.

MESSENGER FROM MARS?

A meteorite found in Antarctica caused a sensation in 1996 when scientists thought there were signs of life inside it. The meteorite was a rare type which is believed to come from the planet Mars. Some scientists thought that photographs taken through a powerful microscope showed tiny 'micro-fossils' inside the meteorite – evidence that very primitive bugs might once have lived on Mars. But other scientists didn't agree. They were not sure that the photos showed bugs at all, and even if they did, they might be Earth-bugs which got into

the meteorite during the thousands of years it lay on the Earth's surface before it was picked up. So we still don't know for sure whether there is any life on Mars, or anywhere else in the solar system.

HOLE IN THE SKY

In 1982 a British scientist working in Antarctica discovered a 'hole in the sky'. Dr Joe Farman was working at a place called Halley Bay. His job was to measure how thick the ozone layer is – a region high up in the atmosphere where ozone gas acts as a shield to protect us from harmful ultraviolet rays from the sun. He found that the ozone shield over Antarctica was getting thinner, forming a huge patch known as the 'ozone hole'. Pollution by gases from spray cans may be the cause of the hole. These gases are not used much now, but it may be years before the ozone shield gets back to full strength.

There are signs that the ozone layer is getting thinner round the North Pole too, with the thinner region even spreading over Europe. So that's another good reason always to protect yourself if you go out in bright sunshine for more than a few minutes.

TALL TALES

Suppose some explorers come back from the South Pole and tell you about the polar bears they saw there. And another explorer, back from a trip to the North Pole, boasts about how nice it was to have a penguin's egg for breakfast. Would you believe their tales? Certainly not, because there are no penguins in the Arctic, and no polar bears in the Antarctic. But if someone says they've been to the Antarctic and seen an Arctic tern, that could be true. Terns are amazing birds that lay their eggs in Arctic regions in the summer, but when the winter starts they fly more than 16,000 kilometres down to the Antarctic.

I DON'T BELIEVE WE'VE EVER MET ...

COLD SPOT

Today the population of the South Pole is sometimes more than 100. Many of the people there are scientists working at the Research Station. A few people stay there for a whole year, but many just visit for the summer, when it stays light continuously for six months and the outdoor temperature can get as high as −14 °C (7 °F) – much the same as in your freezer at home. In winter the temperature can go as low as − 80 °C (−110 °F), with winds of more than 160 kilometres per hour.

WARM UP WITH AN ICE CREAM

Quiz

1   Which of these is *not* true about Antarctica?
    a) It is bigger than Australia
    b) It is a floating island made of ice
    c) You can find meteorites there

2   *Erebus* and *Terror* were the names of . . .
    a) Two of Roald Amundsen's dogs
    b) Sir John Franklin's ships
    c) Two of Robert Scott's ponies

3   Franklin's expedition was searching for . . .
    a) The North-West Passage
    b) The Abominable Snowman
    c) The Ozone Hole

4   You have just seen an igloo and your magnetic compass points
    straight downwards. Where are you?
    a) At the Geographic South Pole
    b) At the Geographic North Pole
    c) At the Magnetic North Pole

5   In 1959 a party of Americans reached the North Pole by . . .
    a) Submarine
    b) Helicopter
    c) Balloon

6   Why did Roald Amundsen change his mind and go to the South Pole
    instead of the North Pole?
    a) Because he thought it wouldn't be so cold
    b) Because he thought someone had already reached the North Pole
    c) Because his ship was blown off course

7   How far from safety were Robert Scott and his companions when
    they died?
    a) More than 2000 kilometres
    b) About 200 kilometres
    c) Less than 20 kilometres

8   The 'Ozone Hole' is
    a) A hole in the ice caused by a meteorite
    b) A change in the atmosphere caused by pollution
    c) A top band from the 1980s

9   Which of these would you *not* expect to see?
    a) A penguin in Antarctica
    b) An Arctic tern in Antarctica
    c) A submarine at the South Pole

10 Which of these *would* you expect to find at the South Pole in
    summer?
    a) A lot of scientists
    b) Total darkness
    c) A herd of polar bears

The boundless ocean

The first sailors stayed close to the shore, creeping from port to port so that they could dash to safety if a storm blew up. But some took bigger risks. Polynesian people island-hopped across the Pacific in large canoes, and Arab traders sailed as far as the Indian Ocean.

Six centuries ago, sailors from Spain, Portugal and other European countries began to make even longer journeys. They crossed the widest oceans in ships that would seem tiny today, often out of sight of land for months at a time. They faced danger from storms and hidden rocks, from starvation when food and water ran out, and even from attack by hostile natives when they found somewhere to land. The reward was the discovery of new continents, such as Australia, and North and South America — places which no one in Europe knew about until Columbus and the other great explorers first went there.

As the new continents were drawn on to maps, other explorers filled in the details. Scientists often travelled with them, ready to go ashore at every port to study the rocks, look for fossils, and collect new animals and plant life.

FIRST COMPASS

The first magnetic compasses were probably made by putting a magnetised needle inside a piece of straw and floating it on a dish of water. The needle turns to line up pointing north-south, pulled into place by the Earth's own magnetism. Before they had compasses, sailors could only find where north is at times when the sky was clear, so that they could watch the movement of the sun across the sky, or look for the Pole Star at night. After the compass came into use, 900 years ago, they could tell which way they were going, even when there were weeks of non-stop cloudy weather.

MAGNETIC MAGIC

Sailors were not allowed to eat onions or garlic at sea, in case the smell on their breath stopped the ship's compass from working. When compasses were first used, many people had strange ideas about them; they thought magnetism was a sort of magic, and were scared of it. They believed that a small piece of magnetic stone, called a lodestone, could cure some illnesses, but the smell of onion or garlic

would destroy its magnetism. And if a husband put the stone under his wife's pillow when she went to bed, she was supposed to wake up and reveal whether she had any secret lovers. But by Columbus' time the compass was so useful that people gradually stopped believing in its possible magical effects.

CROSSING THE ATLANTIC

Christopher Columbus didn't discover America, and his name wasn't Christopher Columbus! But he was still a very great explorer. When he lived in Spain he called himself Cristóbal Colón, but today we use a Latin version of his name, Columbus. When he set off across the Atlantic in 1492, Columbus thought he would soon reach Japan or China. At that time no one in Europe knew there was a huge continent in the way – the one we now call America. Later it was discovered that sailors from Norway had landed in North America nearly 500 years before Columbus. Some of them had even lived there for a few years.

WRONG CALCULATION

If Columbus had got his sums right he might never have set out on his journey of exploration. He knew that the Earth was round, so there should be two ways to go from Spain to Japan – the usual way eastwards through Asia, or a new way westwards across the Atlantic. He worked out that the new way should be quite

short, less than 5000 kilometres, and set out to prove it. But the figures he used were quite wrong. The real distance is about four times further, and Columbus and all his men would have died long before they got to Japan, if they hadn't had the good luck to discover the West Indies instead.

TOO FAR FROM HOME

Columbus kept a false log book so that his men wouldn't find out how far from home they really were. No one had ever sailed straight out to sea for so long, and he didn't want the other people on his expedition to discover they were actually 5000 kilometres from home.

So in the logbook he showed to other people he pretended the distance was shorter than it really was. But he had another, correct, logbook which he kept secret. Even so, after three weeks with no sight of land, his men refused to go any further. They even talked of throwing Columbus overboard and heading home without him. But in the end they agreed to go on for just three more days. Luckily for Columbus they reached land only two days later. Columbus thought they had landed near Japan, but today we know it was an island in the Bahamas. He had discovered a 'new world' without realising it.

WRONG NAME

For 500 years Native Americans have been called by the wrong name – 'Indians'. When Columbus reached land on 12 October 1492 he was sure he was on an island near China or Japan, in a region known as 'The Indies'. So he gave the name 'Indians' to the people he found there. Thirty years later everyone knew that Columbus was wrong. He was nowhere near The Indies, and the so-called Indians were not Indians at all. Today the descendants of people who lived in America before the Europeans

went there are called 'Native Americans'. But the islands which Columbus discovered will always be known as the 'West Indies'.

I NAME THIS COUNTRY...

America might have been named Columbia, after Christopher Columbus. The newly-discovered continent was given its name by a little-known German map-maker, who later changed his mind. The map-maker, called Martin Waldseemúller, may not have known about Columbus' exploits. In a book he wrote in 1507 he said that the new continent should be named after a later explorer, Amerigo Vespucci, and he labelled it 'America' on his maps. Later he decided that he had made a mistake and Vespucci shouldn't really be given the honour of 'discoverer of the New World'. So he had the name 'America' taken off his maps. But by then it was too late. His first maps were so well known that everyone was using the name 'America'.

ROUND THE WORLD VOYAGE

When Ferdinand Magellan set off on his round-the-world expedition in 1517 he took 35 spare magnetic needles, in case the vital one in his compass lost its magnetism. To make sure he knew where he was going, he also took 23 charts, 29 instruments for measuring the position of the Sun and stars, and 18 sand-glasses for measuring time. Even so, when he reached the far side of the world he was 5400 kilometres off course! The expedition also

carried a good supply of mercury, the silvery liquid metal sometimes called quicksilver. This was useful for giving as presents to people on the islands they visited. (Today we know that mercury is poisonous.)

TOUGH EATING

We sometimes say a piece of meat is 'as tough as old boots', but sailors on Magellan's expedition really did eat leather. When food ran out on the three-month crossing of the vast Pacific Ocean, they stripped off sheets of leather used to protect some of the ship's woodwork, soaked it in seawater for a few days to soften it, and then ate it. About 250 men set out on the expedition – including one Englishman. Three years later just eighteen struggled home at the end of the journey. Magellan himself wasn't one of them. He had been killed in a battle on an island which is now part of the Philippines.

NO SMOKING

Until 1565, Britain was a No Smoking zone. Tobacco does not normally grow in Europe, but when Columbus crossed the Atlantic he saw Native Americans smoking pipes. He and other explorers brought back seeds of the tobacco plant, and the habit gradually caught on in Europe. At first tobacco was used as a medicine, to help people relax; it wasn't until much later that people realised that tobacco-smoking also causes serious diseases. It is said that when some of the first smokers in Britain lit up their pipes, their friends thought they were on fire and doused them with water.

UNINHABITED ISLAND

In 1609 Henry Hudson found a pleasant island off the coast of North America, inhabited only by a few Native Americans. Today, more than a million people live on that island. Its name is Manhattan, and it forms the heart of the city of New York. Hudson was a British explorer who sailed up the river that runs alongside Manhattan (now called the Hudson River). He was looking for a short-cut route to India, but had to give up when he didn't find it. A few years later a Dutchman persuaded the Indian chiefs on Manhattan Island to do a deal. He gave them a few bits of cloth and some jewellery, worth about £20. They gave him the entire island of Manhattan in exchange!

LEFT TO DIE

If you're leading an expedition by ship, it pays to keep on good terms with the crew. Henry Hudson forgot this, and it cost him his life. In 1611 Hudson, with his son John, was in his ship *Discovery*, exploring the region of Northern Canada now called Hudson's Bay. Food was running short, and some of the ship's crew thought Hudson was keeping a private hoard of

food for himself and a few friends. Tempers flared, and some of the crew captured Hudson, with his friends and his young son. They put them into a small boat and set them adrift on the open sea. *Discovery* sailed back to England without them, and nothing more was ever heard of Hudson, or his son and his friends.

WHERE IN THE WORLD?

In 1714 the British government offered a huge prize to the first person who could find a way to stop sailors getting lost at sea. The prize was £20,000, worth more than a million pounds in today's money. The problem was that sailors had no easy way of finding out their longitude once they were out of sight of land. A measurement of longitude would tell them how far they had travelled in an east or west direction. Without it, sailors could not be sure where they were. As a result, ships were often wrecked by crashing into rocks unexpectedly.

DISASTER STRIKES

One of the worst disasters happened on a foggy night in October 1707, when a group of warships were returning to England from the

Mediterranean. The person in charge was called Admiral Sir Clowdisley Shovell. It is said that a sailor on one of the ships warned him that his ships were in danger, but Sir Clowdisley thought he knew better. He had the impertinent sailor put to death by hanging – and took no notice of the warning. But the sailor had been right; the ships were off course, and soon four of them ran on to rocks near the Scilly Isles and sank. Two thousand people were drowned.

SOLVING THE PROBLEM

To stop this happening again, the £20,000 prize was offered. Lots of people tried to find ways of winning it. One of the best ideas was to make a very accurate clock, which could be set to the correct time before leaving England, and then carried aboard the ship. Wherever they were in the world, sailors could make measurements to find when the Sun reached its highest position in the sky. By comparing these measurements with the time on the clock brought from England they could work out their longitude, because the further round the Earth you go, the bigger the difference between the time of mid-day at the place where you are, and the time of mid-day back in England. But in 1715

no one had invented a clock that was good enough to work well on board a ship.

BARKING MAD

One of the craziest ideas was to use a dog instead of a clock. A man called Sir Kenelm Digby got hold of some 'magic powder' from France. He claimed that a wounded animal could be healed, just by sprinkling the powder on to one of its bandages. Amazingly, the method was supposed to work even when the

animal and the bandage were far apart, with the animal giving a yelp of pain at exactly the moment when the powder was sprinkled on to its bandage kilometres away. So instead of taking an accurate clock to sea, all you needed was a wounded dog, and a person left behind at home who would sprinkle the powder at exactly 12 noon each day. Keep watching the dog, and when it suddenly yelps for no reason, you know it's 12 noon at home. From this, you can work out your longitude. Needless to say, this crazy idea did not win the prize.

WINNING ENTRY

In the end the £20,000 prize was won by a Yorkshire carpenter called John Harrison, but only after he had spent more than thirty years trying to solve the problem. Harrison built four wonderful clocks, each one better than the last. He invented many improvements to make sure these clocks kept accurate time even when carried on a long voyage over stormy seas. Harrison's fourth clock looked like a giant watch, and was good enough to win him the prize. By then Harrison was eighty years old. (You can see the actual clocks at the Old Royal Observatory at Greenwich, near London.)

CAPTAIN COOK

Who was the greatest explorer ever? Many people say it was Captain James Cook, who was the leader of three great voyages of discovery between 1768 and 1779. He was an expert navigator and map-maker, and sailed right round the world twice. He was the first European to visit Hawaii, New Zealand and eastern Australia – where he was amazed to see

the kangaroos. In Cook's day many people thought there might be an undiscovered 'southern continent' which could be inhabited, but Cook proved that it doesn't exist. Sadly he was killed in Hawaii at the age of 51 when an argument over a stolen boat blew up into a full-scale fight with the native people there.

LIFE-SAVING DIET

Pickled cabbage saved the lives of many sailors on Captain Cook's famous voyages of exploration. Before his time, up to half the sailors who set off on a long voyage might never reach the end. They died from a disease called scurvy, caused by not eating enough fresh food. Captain Cook prevented scurvy by making his men eat pickled cabbage, known as 'sauer-kraut'.

EAT YOUR CABBAGE OR ELSE!

(Today we know that the vital ingredient in sauerkraut is vitamin C). Cook also took live chickens, sheep and pigs on his expeditions so that his men could have fresh eggs and meat – though the pigs soon died of cold.

WATER, WATER EVERYWHERE

People can be surrounded by water but still die of thirst. A good supply of drinking water is more important for staying alive than a supply of food. Shipwrecked sailors soon get thirsty, but the sea-water all around them is no help. It's so salty that drinking it would only make them more thirsty. As the poet Coleridge put it, you can have 'water, water, everywhere, nor any drop to drink'. But Captain Cook's sailors didn't have to worry about thirst. They all got a ration of a gallon of beer (4.5 litres) a day, as well as half a pint of rum (0.3 litres) at lunchtime. The *Endeavour* also carried chemical apparatus which could be used to change sea-water into drinking-water.

KEEPING CLEAN

On Cook's ship, the *Endeavour*, everyone had to wash at least once a week. But they didn't use soap; instead they washed in sea-water and rubbed themselves with pumice – a form of stone that works rather like sandpaper. And

they had to put on clean clothes twice a week. Inside the ship, all wooden surfaces were kept clean by rubbing them with an evil-smelling mixture of vinegar and gunpowder. Cook's enthusiasm for keeping everything clean paid off. On the whole three-year voyage not a single person died from illness caught on the ship.

OVERCROWDED SHIP

Even though *Endeavour* was already overcrowded, Captain Cook agreed to take an extra passenger on his three-year voyage, a scientist called Sir Joseph Banks. But when Banks arrived, it turned out he liked to travel in style, because he brought with him another scientist friend, a secretary, two artists, four servants and two greyhounds, as well as all their luggage and scientific equipment – all of which had to be squeezed on board.

Banks added to the storage problem by collecting more than 30,000 plants during the course of the expedition. More than a thousand of these were new types which no one had ever recorded before. Some of these are plants which people have in their gardens today.

Quiz

1 A lodestone is . . .
   a) A piece of magnetic rock
   b) A very heavy weight
   c) A type of onion

2 When Christopher Columbus crossed the Atlantic in 1492 he was hoping to arrive somewhere near . . .
   a) America
   b) Japan
   c) Australia

3 America is named after . . .
   a) A German mapmaker
   b) A French ship-builder
   c) An Italian explorer

4 Ferdinand Magellan's greatest achievement was . . .
   a) To invent the magnetic compass
   b) To make his sailors eat leather
   c) To lead a round-the-world expedition

5 What bad habit was brought from America to Europe by early explorers?
   a) Drinking coca-cola
   b) Smoking tobacco
   c) Chewing gum

6   In 1609 Henry Hudson discovered
    a) The bay where San Francisco is today
    b) The lost continent of Atlantis
    c) The island where New York is today

7   In 1714 the British government offered a £20,000 prize to the first
    person who could . . .
    a) Stop sailors feeling seasick
    b) Help sailors find their longitude
    c) Raise the *Titanic*

8   The prize was eventually won by
    a) Richard Branson
    b) Bruce Forsyth
    c) John Harrison

9   Captain Cook made his sailors eat pickled cabbage . . .
    a) To keep them healthy
    b) To stop them smelling
    c) As a punishment

10 Captain Cook died at the age of 51 . . .
    a) In a fight with people in Hawaii
    b) When his ship hit the Great Barrier Reef
    c) After being kicked by a kangaroo in Australia

Down in the depths

By the year 1800, three-quarters of our planet's surface still hadn't been explored — that's how much of the Earth is covered by the oceans. Then scientists began to get interested in the underwater world, and explored it by dangling measuring devices on long ropes over the sides of ships. It was the start of a branch of science known as oceanography.

Soon people found ways to go underwater themselves, in submarines and 'diving bells' which let them explore the underwater world with their own eyes. The enemy was always pressure. The deeper you dive below the surface, the more you are crushed by the weight of all the water above you. In places the ocean is several kilometres deep, so the pressure at the bottom is huge. When explorers finally reached the bottom of the deepest ocean on Earth, in 1960, they travelled inside an enormously strong metal ball.

In recent years underwater exploring has revealed huge mountains and valleys on the ocean floor. Colonies of strange creatures have been found which spend their whole lives in the darkness of the ocean bottom, and cannot survive if they are brought up to the surface.

HEAVE HO!

When a sea-captain tried to find how deep the ocean was in 1816 he needed a rope so long that it took 100 men more than an hour to haul it back in. At that time the only method of 'sounding' the ocean (finding its depth) was to lower a cable with a weight on the end from a ship, and measure how much rope had to be paid out before it hit the bottom. Captain Robert Wauchope used a rope 2.6 kilometres long and more than 6 centimetres thick, weighted down with cannon balls. So it's no surprise that he needed 100 men, sweating away for an hour and 20 minutes, to haul it all back in.

BATS SHOW HOW

When humans began to copy bats they found a much easier way to measure the depth of the oceans. Many bats do not use their eyes. Instead they send out high-pitched squeaks of sound. By listening for the echoes which bounce back from anything in front of them, the bats can find their food and avoid crashing into obstacles. In the 1920s, ocean explorers began to use the same technique, called

echo-sounding. They made a 'ping' of sound by hitting the metal of the ship's hull with a hammer, and listened for the echo made by the sound bouncing back from the sea-bed. The deeper the ocean, the longer it takes for the echo to come back. So by timing the echo they could work out how deep the water is.

HANGING BY A THREAD

In 1934 two Americans trusted their lives to a steel cable less than 2.5 centimetres thick and nearly a kilometre in length. William Beebe and Otis Barton were underwater explorers. They climbed through a hole only 35 centimetres across to get inside a steel ball called a bathy-sphere. Then the 2.5 tonne bathysphere was lowered into the ocean on a cable suspended from a ship on the surface. Beebe and Barton looked out through port-holes made of quartz 7.5 centimetres thick as their tiny cabin was lowered to a record-breaking depth of 923 metres. If the cable had snapped, the bathy-sphere would have sunk to the bottom like a lead weight.

LIFE AT THE BOTTOM

Can anything survive at the bottom of the deepest oceans? This question was answered on 23 January 1960, when Jacques Piccard and Don Walsh reached the bottom of the deepest ocean on Earth in their bathyscaphe *Trieste* (a sort of submarine). In the chilly blackness of the ocean bottom their searchlights picked out the grey shape of a fish, about 45 centimetres long. With two round eyes on the top of its head, the fish glared at the invading bathy-scaphe for a few moments before swimming slowly away. It was surviving at a place where the water pressure is 1 tonne on every square centimetre of its body. So what sort of fish was it? At that pressure, a *flat*fish of course!

DEEP WATER

Imagine a pool of water so deep it would completely cover the Sears Tower skyscraper, which is 110 storeys high. Now imagine water so deep it would cover 25 Sears Towers, one on top of another. That's the depth of the deepest ocean on Earth. It's called the Challenger Deep, because it was discovered by the British survey ship called HMS *Challenger II*. Challenger Deep

is part of the Marianas Trench in the Pacific Ocean. Nine years after it was discovered, Piccard and Walsh took their bathyscaphe to the bottom of Challenger Deep. Going down was like being in a lift, except that it took more than five hours to complete the downward journey of almost 11 kilometres.

DIVING BALL

200,000 tonnes of water pressed on the outside of Piccard and Walsh's cabin when their bathyscaphe *Trieste* was at the bottom of its historic descent into Challenger Deep. That's the weight of all the water up above the cabin, weighing down on it. But the two explorers were safe, because their tiny cabin was a steel ball designed to stand up to such high pressure. The cabin was attached to a much larger buoyancy tank, filled with petrol. Petrol is lighter than water, so the buoyancy tank could provide the lifting force needed to bring the bathyscaphe back up to the surface. *Trieste* wasn't attached to the surface by a cable, and could move around freely under its own power, like a submarine.

ALVIN EXPLORES THE DEEP

For thirty years teams of scientists have explored the bottom of the sea from a submersible named after a cartoon chipmunk. The chipmunk was called *Alvin* (which is also a short version of the name of the scientist, Allyn Vine, who first suggested the sub should be built). *Alvin* – the submersible – is a mini-submarine, about the size of a bus. It is so strongly built that it can go ten times deeper under water than normal submarines can, its three passengers protected from the water pressure by a sealed cabin made of ultra-strong titanium metal 5 centimetres thick.

JETS, WORMS AND SMELLY GAS

In the 1970s, scientists in *Alvin* were amazed to discover jets of boiling hot water spurting out from the bottom of the sea. This water is more than three times hotter than water boiling in a saucepan at home, but the huge pressure three kilometres underwater stops it turning to steam. The scientists were even more astonished at what *Alvin*'s searchlights picked out around the

water jets: giant white worms, shaped like tubes as thick as your leg, and up to two metres long. There's no sunlight, and no normal food so deep in the ocean, so the tube-worms get their energy from evil-smelling sulphur gas dissolved in the boiling water.

SOGGY SANDWICHES

By 1996 *Alvin* had made more than 3000 dives, including one unexpected one when the sub was accidentally dropped into 1500 metres of

water and sank to the bottom. Luckily the pilot, Ed Bland, escaped from the sub before it sank, but left his packed lunch inside. *Alvin* lay on the sea floor for nearly a year. When it was finally rescued by another submersible, Ed Bland's sandwiches were found to be 'soggy but edible'. Other excitements in *Alvin's* eventful life include finding a nuclear missile which had been accidentally dropped into the sea near Spain, and photographing the wreck of the great ocean liner *Titanic*, lying in the deep Atlantic since it sank it 1912.

GOING NOWHERE

In 1960, 183 Americans set out on a voyage of exploration. Three months later they had travelled 50,000 kilometres, but they ended where they started, and saw absolutely nothing on the way! The men were sailors in an American submarine, the USS *Triton*, on the first-ever round-the-world underwater voyage. The sub could stay underwater for so long because it was driven by nuclear power, so it didn't need to refuel (in fact it could have gone round the world four times without refuelling). And the men didn't suffocate because electricity

from the nuclear reactor was used to make oxygen out of water for them to breathe.

THE SHIP WITH THE HOLE

A ship was built in the 1970s with a hole in the middle the size of a football field. Special cranes could raise things from the bottom of the sea through this huge hole. The ship was called the *Glomar Explorer* and cost 350 million dollars to build. The people who built it pretended it would be used for exploring the bottom of the Pacific Ocean, and dredging up valuable metal lumps called nodules that are found there.

But the *Glomar Explorer* really had a quite different and sinister purpose. It was built for the American spy agency, the CIA, specially to bring up from the bottom of the sea a Russian submarine that had sunk there by accident in 1968. That was why it needed such a large hole in the middle – big enough for an entire submarine to be lifted through. It is said that the submarine was brought up successfully but broke in two before it was lifted aboard the *Explorer*.

MONSTER OF THE DEEP

In the 1990s scientists are still searching for a sea monster twice the size of a bus, called a giant squid. It is an octopus-like creature, with tentacles, a long beak, and eyes the size of dinner-plates. We know that some whales catch giant squids and eat them, because the squids' beaks have been found in the stomachs of dead whales. Giant squids do really exist, because dead ones have been washed up on beaches in several different parts of the world, but no one has ever seen a live one and no one knows where they live. So watch out next time you go swimming at the seaside!

Quiz

1　A bathysphere is . . .
   a) A circular jacuzzi
   b) An underwater cinema
   c) A ball used by divers

2　An echo-sounder is . . .
   a) A device for frightening away dangerous fish
   b) A device for measuring how deep the sea is
   c) A burglar-alarm used on ships

3　At the bottom of the Marianas Trench, Piccard and Walsh
  discovered . . .
   a) A flatfish
   b) A Russian submarine
   c) An empty Coke can

4　The cabin that deep sea divers travel in needs to be very strong, to
  protect them from . . .
   a) Being crushed by the huge water pressure
   b) Being swallowed by a whale
   c) Colliding with shipwrecks

5　A submersible is a . . .
   a) Baby submarine
   b) Baby chipmunk
   c) Scientist who studies fish

6. Where would you look for a giant white worm, up to two metres long?
   a) In the tropical rainforest
   b) In a giant's garden
   c) At the bottom of the ocean

7. Which of these is *not* the name of a craft used for underwater exploration?
   a) *Alvin*
   b) *Emu*
   c) *Trieste*

8. What can go round the world four times without refuelling?
   a) A Boeing 747
   b) An Arctic tern
   c) A nuclear submarine

9. Nodules are . . .
   a) Characters in a cartoon
   b) Metal lumps from the bottom of the sea
   c) Baby penguins

10. Scientists think that one of these creatures really exists. Which one?
    a) A giant watersnake called the Loch Ness Monster
    b) An octopus-like creature called a Giant Squid
    c) A shark-like creature called Jaws

The sky above

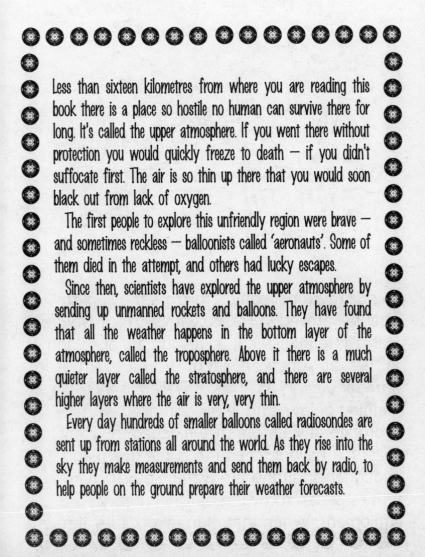

Less than sixteen kilometres from where you are reading this book there is a place so hostile no human can survive there for long. It's called the upper atmosphere. If you went there without protection you would quickly freeze to death — if you didn't suffocate first. The air is so thin up there that you would soon black out from lack of oxygen.

The first people to explore this unfriendly region were brave — and sometimes reckless — balloonists called 'aeronauts'. Some of them died in the attempt, and others had lucky escapes.

Since then, scientists have explored the upper atmosphere by sending up unmanned rockets and balloons. They have found that all the weather happens in the bottom layer of the atmosphere, called the troposphere. Above it there is a much quieter layer called the stratosphere, and there are several higher layers where the air is very, very thin.

Every day hundreds of smaller balloons called radiosondes are sent up from stations all around the world. As they rise into the sky they make measurements and send them back by radio, to help people on the ground prepare their weather forecasts.

TROUSERLESS JOURNEY

The first two balloonists to cross the English
Channel arrived in France without their trousers.
Jean-Pierre Blanchard, a Frenchman, and John
Jeffries, an American, set off from Dover Castle
on 7 January 1785. They travelled in a basket
hanging below a huge balloon filled with
hydrogen gas. Before they reached the French
coast the balloon began to come down and was
in danger of hitting the water. So Blanchard and
Jeffries began throwing out their heavy
equipment. When that didn't work they threw

out their jackets and trousers as well. At last the balloon began to rise, and brought the near-naked aeronauts to a safe landing near Calais. The French King awarded the Frenchman a large cash prize for his brave achievement, but the American got nothing.

SUMMER SNOW

When a French scientist explored the atmosphere high above Paris, he found snowflakes, even though it was midsummer. The scientist, J A Barral, made his record breaking balloon ascent on a July day in 1850. His friend A J Bixio came along for the ride, and they took with them a thermometer to measure the temperature and a barometer to measure air pressure. After climbing for an hour they reached a height of seven kilometres, where their balloon was surrounded by a thin high ice cloud (now called a cirrus cloud). The thermometer reading plummeted to -39 °C – much colder than in your freezer at home – and a swarm of fine ice crystals surrounded the balloon. Barral and Bixio soon came back to Earth, where it was still a warm summer's day.

SAVED BY HIS TEETH

A Victorian scientist was saved from death in
the upper atmosphere by his assistant's teeth.
The scientist, James Glaisher, made his first
balloon ascent in September 1862. At first
all went well. Glaisher made scientific
measurements while his assistant, Henry
Coxwell, controlled the balloon. Three
kilometres up they burst out of the clouds into
the blue sky and sunshine above. The balloon
was still rising fast, and after two hours of flight
Glaisher and Coxwell were eight kilometres up,
higher than anyone had ever gone before. Now
their troubles began.

GOOD THINKING

As they passed the ten-kilometre mark, Glaisher
found his eye-sight failing. A few minutes later
he could no longer move his arms or legs, and
a minute or two after that he became
unconscious, his body paralysed by cold and
lack of oxygen. Coxwell realised it was time to
come down. But when he tried to pull the string
that would let gas out of the balloon, he found
his arms were paralysed too. The only chance
was to grab the string in his teeth. At the third

attempt he succeeded, and soon the balloon was on its way down. Both men had fully recovered by the time they landed. The whole historic flight had taken only two and a half hours.

GAS BAGS

Oxygen stored in a bag made from cows' intestines saved the life of a French balloonist in 1875. Paul Bert, a scientist and politician, wanted to test his idea that mountaineers and balloonists could survive better at high levels by taking a supply of oxygen to breathe. But how could they carry the gas in the days before plastic bags had been invented? Bags made from the intestines of cows were the answer. So two of Bert's friends went up in a balloon to test the idea, but they left it too late, and one of them died before he could use the oxygen. Bert's basic idea was a good one, and oxygen gas – from cylinders – has been used by thousands of mountaineers, balloonists and high-flying pilots since that time.

ON TOP OF THE WORLD

In 1897 three men and thirty-six pigeons set off to reach the North Pole by balloon. It was 1930 before anyone knew whether they ever got there. The party's leader was a Swedish engineer, Salomon Andrée. With two other men, he set off from a small island north of

Norway, carried by a vast balloon called *Ornen* (Swedish for *Eagle*). Their luggage included tents, boats and sledges in case they crash-landed, and three months' supply of food. Radio had not been invented, so the pigeons were intended for sending back messages, carried in tiny tins hidden in the birds' tail feathers.

BY BALLOON TO THE POLE

On 11 July 1897, to the cheers of people on the ground, *Ornen* began its 1100-kilometre journey to the Pole. But even at the start there was trouble. To steer the balloon, long ropes called draglines dangled from it on to the ice below. As *Ornen* was launched some of these draglines broke loose. Soon the three explorers disappeared over the horizon, but with little control over where their balloon would take them. Nothing was heard from them until four days later, when an unusual bird settled on a fishing boat that happened to be in the region. It was one of *Ornen's* pigeons, with a note from Salomon Andrée to say that the flight was going well. The message was dated 13 July, two days after launch. No later messages were ever received.

REMAINS IN THE ICE

The end of the story came more than 30 years later. On a remote island in the Arctic Ocean, sailors from a seal-hunting ship saw strange black objects sticking out of the snow. It was the remains of a camp, complete with cooking utensils and a stove that still worked. Nearby, they found three skeletons, and some hand-written diaries. The sailors had stumbled on the place where Salomon Andrée and his two companions had died. The diaries told the story of what had happened.

POISONED BY BEAR MEAT?

For three days the balloon had travelled over desolate ice and water. Freezing fog weighed it down with ice, and it slowly lost gas. Long before they reached the Pole, the balloon came down and was dragged bumping along the ice by the wind. The three explorers had to abandon the balloon, and set off on a 400-kilometre trek over floating ice to safety. For three months they had trudged along, until finally they reached the island where their remains were eventually found. Nobody knows why they died there, because they were not

short of food. On the journey they had shot polar bears for meat, and one theory is that they ate too much of the bears' livers, without realising that they are poisonous. Or perhaps it was simply the cold and exhaustion that killed them.

CATHEDRAL IN THE AIR

A balloon launched in 1960 was bigger than St Paul's Cathedral. It didn't carry people, but scientific apparatus used to study cosmic rays

(particles – smaller than atoms – that hit the Earth's atmosphere from outer space). The balloon was made of plastic and filled with helium gas. It rose to a height of 36 kilometres. An extra-large balloon was needed because the air at this height is very thin, so the lifting-power of a balloon is much less than it is at lower levels.

BALLOONS FOR SCIENCE

Have you ever launched a helium balloon at a fête and wondered where it will end up? Usually these balloons only stay up a few hours and don't travel further than a few hundred kilometres. But unmanned balloons launched by scientists to study the atmosphere do much better. They can stay up for more than a year, and sometimes drift right round the world. Other balloons don't stay up so long, but are designed to go as high as possible. They can carry loads of complex equipment to a height of 42 kilometres, which is above 99.8 per cent of the atmosphere. These balloons are sometimes used to test equipment that will later be flown on a satellite.

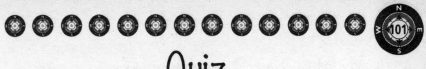
Quiz

1   The stratosphere is . . .
    a) The bottom layer of the atmosphere
    b) A higher layer of the atmosphere
    c) A football stadium in Brazil

2   Which of these did the Frenchman J-P Blanchard throw out of his
    balloon in 1785?
    a) His trousers
    b) His gold watch
    c) His companion, John Jeffries

3   As you go up in a balloon the conditions change. Which of these is
    not true?
    a) The air pressure goes up
    b) The amount of oxygen goes down
    c) The temperature goes down

4   Which record did James Glaisher and Henry Coxwell break in 1862?
    a) Going furthest in a balloon
    b) Going highest in a balloon
    c) Olympic balloon-throwing record

5   What did two French balloonists take up inside a bag made from
    cows' intestines in 1875?
    a) Hydrogen gas
    b) Oxygen gas
    c) Brandy

6   Why did the explorer Salomon Andrée take pigeons on his balloon?
    a) For making pigeon pie
    b) To provide a supply of eggs
    c) For carrying messages

7   Why is it a bad idea to rely on polar bear meat for food in the
    Arctic?
    a) Because some of it is poisonous
    b) Because it tastes horrid
    c) Because polar bears are too fierce to catch

8   Why did a huge balloon carry scientific equipment to a great height
    in 1960?
    a) To take photographs of the Earth
    b) To look for rare birds
    c) To study particles from outer space

9   The highest that balloons have gone in the atmosphere is
    a) More than 40 kilometres
    b) More than 400 kilometres
    c) To the Moon

10 The furthest a balloon has travelled is
    a) From England to France
    b) From America to Europe
    c) Right round the world

The hidden world

Many modern explorers are scientists who work like detectives. They use clever methods to explore the hidden world of places we can't see or visit directly — like the inside of the Earth. No one has ever been far inside our planet, but scientists have used clues from earthquakes to work out what it would be like if they could go there. Scientists called geophysicists make their own small earthquakes, and use them to work out the best places to drill for oil.

Medical scientists have many cunning ways of exploring what is happening inside our bodies — without having to cut us open first. Simply listening with a stethoscope was the first method, but since then X-ray machines and other complicated gadgets have helped. One of these even lets doctors 'see' the thoughts inside our heads!

Other scientists are time-travellers, who use their skills to explore the past. They can't go back into the past themselves, of course, but they have many clever ways to find out how old things are, like bones, fossils and even bits of rock. Other experiments help them work out what the weather was like on our planet thousands — or even millions — of years ago.

INSIDE THE EARTH

If you want to explore the inside of the Earth, wait for an earthquake. Earthquakes send out vibrations that travel through the Earth. In 1909 a scientist in Yugoslavia timed how long it took for the vibrations from an earthquake to reach different places up to 800 kilometres away. From his results he worked out that the Earth must have a thin outer crust that is different from the layers underneath. Other scientists decided to name the bottom of the crust after its discoverer. The trouble is that his name was Andrija Mohorovicic, and saying 'Mohorovicic discontinuity' is a bit of a tongue-twister, so most people call it the 'Moho' for short.

DEEPEST HOLE

Why not dig a hole to find out what the Earth is like inside? Scientists have tried it, but the deepest hole they managed to drill was only twelve kilometres deep. That didn't even get through the Earth's outermost skin, the 'Crust'. In fact, on a scale model of the Earth one metre across, this deepest-ever hole would be less than one millimetre deep. Volcanoes sometimes

throw out rocks that show us what the Earth is like inside, but even these only come from a few hundred kilometres below the surface.

MAKE YOUR OWN QUAKE

You could die of boredom waiting for an earthquake to happen, so explorers often make their own. Scientists searching for oil make miniature earthquakes, either by drilling a hole in the ground and letting off an explosion inside it, or by using a 'thumper' – a machine that

bangs on the ground, like stamping your foot but much harder. Then they use 'geophones' dotted around the countryside to pick up the vibrations that come through the ground from these man-made quakes. By comparing the different patterns of vibration picked up by the geophones they can work out a lot about the rock structures underground.

SEARCHING FOR OIL

Want to know if your garden would be a good place to drill for oil? One way to find out would be to fly over it in an aeroplane. An instrument called a magnetometer, carried in the plane, can pick up tiny changes in the strength of the Earth's magnetism as it flies from place to place. This gives a clue about the underground rocks, because some rocks are more magnetic than others.

From clues like this, and other information, scientists work out what sort of rocks lie underground, and pick out the best places to drill for oil.

WEIGHED DOWN BY ROCKS

When you stand on the bathroom scales, how much you weigh depends on what rocks lie underneath your house. Heavy rocks pull you downwards with a bit of extra gravity force, compared to lighter rocks. So when you are in a place with heavy rocks under it you weigh more than when you are somewhere with light rocks under it. But the difference is very small, less than the weight of a single postage stamp!

Scientists use instruments called gravimeters to detect tiny changes in the strength of gravity from place to place. From their measurements they can discover things about rocks that are hidden deep underground.

THERE MUST BE SOME VERY HEAVY ROCKS UNDER HERE.

EXPLORING INSIDE OURSELVES

Today we all know someone who has had an X-ray, perhaps to see if a bone is broken or to look for holes in their teeth. But when X-rays were first discovered people could hardly believe that it was actually possible to see right through solid things. One famous scientist, Lord Kelvin, thought it must all be a hoax – but soon had to change his mind. A shop in London started to advertise 'X-ray-proof underwear', but that really was a hoax. To keep X-rays out you would have to wear underclothes made from sheets of lead, which would be like wearing a suit of armour, but much heavier.

X-RAYING A MUMMY

It isn't just modern people who are X-rayed; ancient Egyptian mummies have been X-rayed too. Mummies are the preserved bodies of people (and sometimes cats) who lived about 3000 years ago, wrapped up in bandages. Using X-rays, scientists can explore inside the mummy without undoing the bandages, which might make the mummy crumble away to dust.

By building up three-dimensional X-ray photographs of the teeth of one of the mummies in the British Museum, scientists were able to work out that the ancient Egyptian was only about twenty years old when she died.

CATS AND PETS

You can find CATs and PETs in today's hospitals. They're both ways of exploring inside people without doing them any harm. CAT stands for 'Computerised Axial Tomography' (but don't

worry about that; most people just call it a 'scan'). Lots of narrow beams of X-rays are shone through a person in many different directions. From the results a computer can build up a picture of a cross-section, like a slice, through the person. This is often more useful to doctors than an ordinary X-ray because it is sharper and shows more detail.

SEEING YOUR THOUGHTS

PET is a way of exploring what happens inside a person's brain, without having to open their skull. The letters stand for 'Positron Emission Tomography'. It shows which part of the brain is working hard at any given moment – one part when you are reading a book, for example, and another when you are doing a sum in your head. The human brain is one of the most complicated things in the universe, and the PET method is one way scientists are trying to discover how it works. Teachers would probably prefer to use the PET method to find out whether their pupils are learning mathematics or thinking about what they did last weekend.

EXPLORING THE PAST

Many people have dreamt of time machines that would take them back into the past or forward to the future. It's the story behind a lot of books, films and TV serials. But have you thought what would happen if you really did go back into the past? Suppose you went back 50 years, and by accident you killed your own grandfather – before he had any children. That means you yourself wouldn't ever be born, so you *couldn't* go back in time and kill your

grandfather after all. It simply doesn't make sense. But even if real time travel is impossible, scientists have invented many ways to explore the past without actually going there. You can find out about some of them in the next few pages.

TICKING CLOCK

When it dies, every living thing becomes a special sort of ticking clock, which gradually runs down. By listening to the ticking, from an ancient piece of wood for example, scientists can tell how much the clock has run down. That way they can find how long it is since the tree that the piece of wood comes from was chopped down.

The 'ticking' is made by radioactive atoms of carbon-14 inside the piece of wood, picked up as individual clicks by special detectors of radioactivity. When the tree has just died or been chopped down, each gram of carbon in it makes about four clicks every minute. But when the wood is 6000 years old it only makes two clicks a minute. This way of exploring the past is called 'carbon dating'.

STONE AGE

There are other ways of finding how old something is. Here's one which can be used to find the age of a piece of stone. You may think stones are rather boring things because they don't do much. But in fact there's something going on all the time inside many stones. Very, very gradually, atoms of potassium-40 are changing into atoms of argon-40. The process starts as soon as the stone forms out of melted rock. Then as time goes on the amount of potassium-40 in the stone gets steadily less and the amount of argon-40 gets steadily more. So by measuring how much of each sort of atom there is left in the stone, scientists can find how old it is. The answer is usually measured in millions of years.

LOOKING AT TREE RINGS

TWO THOUSAND, NINE HUNDRED AND TWELVE
TWO THOUSAND, NINE HUNDRED AND THIRTEEN
TWO THOUSAND, NINE HUNDRED AND FOURTEEN
TWO THOUSAND....

How can we find out what the weather was like, hundreds or thousand of years ago? One way is by looking at tree-rings. You've probably counted the rings in a log or a tree-stump to see how old it is, but have you ever looked to see how *thick* each ring is? The rings show how much fatter the tree grows each year. If the year

is very warm or wet, the tree will grow a lot and the rings will be fatter than usual. But an unusually cold or dry year gives extra-narrow rings. So tree rings give a clue to how the climate has changed over the life of the tree. By studying the very old bristle-cone pine trees of North America, for example, scientists have discovered that there was an extra-cold spell of weather about 3000 years ago.

ANCIENT ICE

'Ice-lollies' more than a kilometre long help scientists find out about the weather thousands of years ago. The 'lollies' come from places such as Greenland and Antarctica, where the ground is permanently covered by a very thick layer of ice that has built up over many years. A special drill cuts into the ice and pulls out a long cylinder called an 'ice core' – rather like pulling the cork out of a wine bottle. By studying the frozen core very carefully scientists can work out how the weather has changed over the time it took for the ice layer to form. They can even test tiny bubbles of air, trapped inside the ice, to see what the atmosphere was like all those years ago.

TRAPPED IN AMBER

Twenty-five million years ago, an insect got stuck in the sticky yellow resin oozing out of a tree in Central America. How do we know? Because today that same insect, perfectly preserved, is in a Museum in America where scientists can study it. Trapped in the resin all those years ago, the insect soon died, but the resin turned to a harder material, amber, which has protected the insect ever since. Unlike fossils, which usually only show the bones and shells of long-ago creatures turned into stone, lumps of amber preserve the actual creature itself.

Scientists can open the amber and study the insect in detail, comparing it with the insects that live today. It's one of the best ways scientists have to explore the wild-life of long ago.

But they probably won't ever be able to bring these ancient creatures back to life. So even if you've seen the film of Jurassic Park, you needn't have nightmares about meeting a real-life dinosaur in your back garden.

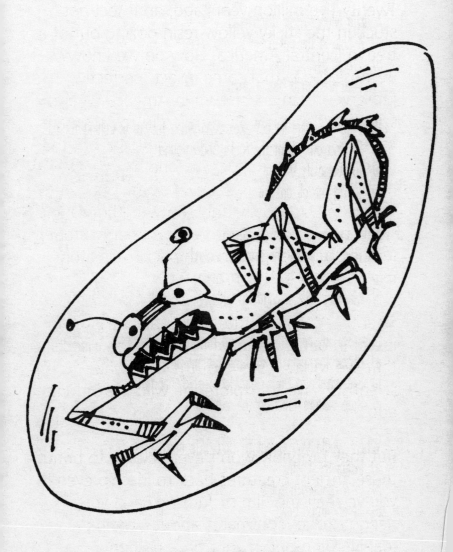

Quiz

1 Andrija Mohorovicic discovered . . .
   a) A hole in the Earth
   b) Where earthquakes come from
   c) That the Earth has a crust

2 Why do scientists let off explosions when they're searching for oil?
   a) To find out about the rocks underground
   b) To scare off birds
   c) To set the oil on fire

3 A gravimeter is a gadget which . . .
   a) Tells you when the gravy's cooked
   b) Measures the height of mountains
   c) Measures the strength of gravity

4 Scientists at the British Museum have used X-rays to . . .
   a) Check the teeth of an Egyptian mummy
   b) See what's in their sandwiches at dinner-time
   c) Stop visitors touching the exhibits

5 Where would you expect to find CATs and PETs?
   a) Inside the Earth
   b) In a modern hospital
   c) At an Arctic base

6 You can find the age of a piece of wood by . . .
  a) Weighing it
  b) Burning it
  c) Testing it for radioactivity

7 By measuring radioactive atoms in stones, scientists can find out . . .
  a) When the world will end
  b) How old the stone is
  c) Who's going to win the lottery

8 One way that scientists can find what the weather was like centuries ago is by . . .
  a) Measuring tree rings
  b) Hanging up a piece of seaweed
  c) Asking a very old weather man

9 What do scientists find inside ice cores?
  a) Penguins' eggs
  b) Tiny lumps of ice-cream
  c) Tiny bubbles of ancient air

10 Where might you find an insect that is 25 million years old?
  a) Under a 25 million-year-old stone
  b) In a piece of amber
  c) On the Moon

NO MORE EXPLORING?

In the 1990s no explorer need ever get lost, anywhere on Earth. By carrying a small receiver, smaller than a walkman, anyone can find out where they are, whenever they want, to an accuracy of about ten metres. The receiver picks up signals from special satellites orbiting overhead, and uses them to work out where it is. It's called the Global Positioning System and you can use it anywhere — on land or sea, even in your own house or garden.

But this doesn't mean there's no more exploring to do. There's still plenty of work for scientific explorers, inventing ways — like the things in the last chapter — to see inside the 'hidden world' where humans can't go for themselves.

And what about explorers who want to travel the world? Well, naturalists are sure there are thousands more species of plants, insects and other creatures, lurking in out-of-the-way places, just waiting for someone to come along and 'discover' them. Who knows — if you were the first person to find a new species and record all its details, it might even be named after you.

So if you want to do some real exploring yourself one day, there will still be plenty of choice!

Quiz Answers

CHAPTER 1 (P 34)

1 - b, 2 - a, 3 - b, 4 - a, 5 - c,
6 - b, 7 - a, 8 - c, 9 - c, 10 - c

CHAPTER 2 (P 53)

1 - b, 2 - b, 3 - a, 4 - c, 5 - a
6 - b, 7 - c, 8 - b 9 - c, 10 - a

CHAPTER 3 (P 76)

1 - a, 2 - b, 3 - c, 4 - c, 5 - b,
6 - c, 7 - b, 8 - c, 9 - a, 10 - a

CHAPTER 4 (P 89)

1 - c, 2 - b, 3 - a, 4 - a, 5 - a,
6 - c, 7 - b, 8 - c, 9 - b, 10 - b

CHAPTER 5 (P 101)

1 - b, 2 - a, 3 - a, 4 - b, 5 - b,
6 - c, 7 - a, 8 - c, 9 - a, 10 - c

CHAPTER 6 (P 118)

1 - c, 2 - a, 3 - c, 4 - a, 5 - b,
6 - c, 7 - b, 8 - a, 9 - c, 10 - b

Index

If you have enjoyed this book, look out for:

THE SCIENCE MUSEUM BOOK OF AMAZING FACTS

DISCOVERIES

Beverley Birch

For trailblazers – a feast of weird and wonderful facts
about discovery – old and new.
Rotting sugarbeet gave the first clues to the
causes of killer diseases.
A small girl playing in caves found Ice Age
paintings over 17,000 years old.
Radioactivity first revealed itself on a cloudy day
in Paris – in a desk drawer.
Peering into rainwater puddles, a curious
linen-draper discovered the invisible world of living
creatures that surrounds us.

If you have enjoyed this book, look out for:

THE SCIENCE MUSEUM BOOK OF AMAZING FACTS

CONSTRUCTIONS

Chris Oxlade

For towering intellects – a feast of weird and
wonderful facts about constructions!
Mosquitoes brought the building of the
Panama Canal to a standstill.
The suspension cables of New York's Brooklyn Bridge
contain enough steel wire to stretch across the
Atlantic four times.
Tunnelling machines owe their design to the teredo
worm, which burrows through damp wood.
The Great Pyramid held the record for the world's
tallest building for nearly four thousand years.

If you have enjoyed this book, look out for:

THE SCIENCE MUSEUM
BOOK OF AMAZING FACTS

TRANSPORT

Beverley Birch

For whizz kids – a feast of weird
and wonderful facts about transport!
The first air passengers were a sheep, a duck
and a cock, who sailed up in a hot air balloon,
watched by the King of France.
In 1838 the fastest journey across the Atlantic
(by steamship) took 15 days. Now Concorde can fly
the distance in 3 hours.
An American inventor has designed a bike with
54 speeds, 5 computers, a security system, a speech
synthesiser, a telephone, and a microfiche file.

If you have enjoyed this book, look out for:

THE SCIENCE MUSEUM
BOOK OF AMAZING FACTS

INVENTIONS

Beverley Birch

For bright sparks – a feast of weird
and wonderful facts about inventions.
The inventors of the first robot were put
on trial for witchcraft.
In the 1700s, dead men's teeth, taken from skulls in
graveyards and battlefields, were used as false teeth.
The first electric light bulbs needed a health warning:
'Do not try and light with a match.'
The first working television was made
from a knitting needle, the lid of a hatbox,
an electric fan motor, and torch batteries, all put
together on top of an old tea-chest.

If you have enjoyed this book, look out for:

THE SCIENCE MUSEUM
BOOK OF AMAZING FACTS

SPACE

Anthony Wilson

For cosmic kids – a feast of weird
and wonderful facts about space!
The footprints that Neil Armstrong left on
the Moon will still be there in a million years.
Some of the atoms in your body are almost
as old as the universe.
When dinosaurs roamed the Earth, there were
only twenty-three and a half hours in a day.
Travelling at the speed of Concorde, a trip to the
nearest star would take 1.5 million years.